the little book of
MANTRAS

MIX
Paper | Supporting responsible forestry
FSC® C144853

Published in 2024 by OH!
An Imprint of Welbeck Non-Fiction Limited,
part of Welbeck Publishing Group.
Offices in: London – 20 Mortimer Street, London W1T 3JW
and Sydney – Level 17, 207 Kent St, Sydney NSW 2000 Australia
www.welbeckpublishing.com

ISBN 978-1-80069-199-5

Editorial consultant: Katalin Patnaik
Editorial: Victoria Denne
Project manager: Russell Porter
Production: Jess Brisley

A CIP catalogue record for this book is available from the British Library

Printed in China

10 9 8 7 6 5 4 3 2 1

the little book of
MANTRAS

katalin patnaik

CONTENTS

INTRODUCTION

Mantras are sacred syllables, words, and phrases that affect a person's state of mind, body, spirit, and even their surroundings.

Chanting mantras brings innumerable benefits. Mantras can calm or energize the mind, heal many diseases that have their root in emotional imbalance, and help the seeker manifest their heart's desire.

Mantras, if they come from pure devotion and a clean heart, can open up spiritual channels to the gods, and bring down their blessings on the practitioner.

The earliest mantras were composed in Vedic Sanskrit, in India, three to four thousand years ago.

The meaning of the word mantra comes from the two syllables it's made up of: man-, meaning mind, and -tra, meaning tool.

A mantra is literally a tool of the mind.

But how do mantras work?

Do mantras rely on the placebo effect? Are they effective because we trick our minds to do the work?

That could be the case, if all mantras had a meaning, but that is not true. Many mantras, especially the beej, seed mantras that are made of a single syllable, do not have any meaning, yet they affect physical reality profoundly.

There are countless examples of how sound affects physical objects, from the soprano shattering glass with her voice, to the story of the Battle of Jericho in the Bible, where the Israelites broke down the city's walls by blowing their trumpets.

There is no question about the effectiveness of sound waves, and how specific frequencies have specific capabilities.

Traditional mantras have very specific resonances tailored to specific needs.

According to Einstein's Law of Vibration, the whole universe is made up of vibrations. Seemingly solid matter, light, and sound. Everything is made up of different frequencies, even us humans.

The universe does not care about the meaning a series of sounds carries – that is already lost when you cross borders to a country with a different language. "I am calm" means nothing to someone who doesn't understand English. But traditional mantras work on a different level. They aren't only psychological tools, but tools that affect physical reality through their vibrations, whether or not one understands or believes in them.

When we think of mantras, Hinduism or Buddhism come to mind, but in fact, every religion and every culture uses mantras, sacred chants, or affirmations in one way or another.

In Abrahamic religions, people say "Amen" at the end of prayers to manifest the prayer's intention.

"So mote it be," say the Wiccans.

"Maranatha," said early Christians,

"Adonai Hineni," chant Jews.

But are mantras religious chants?

Not necessarily. Humans all around the world have realized that words have power, and you don't have to belong to a specific religion to utilize it.

It is also worth mentioning that even if you chant names of Hindu deities, believing in gods as actual entities isn't required – although it is an advantage.

The names of Hindu gods, and the mantras associated with them, have the vibration, the essence of their power.

When you chant the name of a god, you can tap into its archetypical energy, and utilize it in your own life, even if you don't actually believe the god exists.

Of course, if you want to ask specific gods for their blessings, it helps if you worship those gods.

Thinking of gods as individual entities helps to focus your intent, and makes mantras more personal, too.

Chanting the names of gods creates a personal bond between you and the god, which provides a sense of calm and stability in your life. It reinforces the feeling of protection and that everything happens for the best, even if things are rough at the moment.

It can free your mind from suffering, help you see the bigger picture, and trust the process.

The use of affirmations enjoys great popularity today. Many celebrities and successful business people use them to ensure their mindset is right for achieving their goals. Jim Carrey, Oprah, Jennifer Lopez, and Denzel Washington are all firm believers in the effectiveness of affirmations.

Affirmations are the modern-day cousins of mantras. In pop culture, they too are referred to as mantras, although there is an important distinction between the two.

Affirmations are psychological tools
that rely on the words' meanings,
while mantras work on the subatomic,
vibrational level, even if you don't
understand what you are chanting.
Both can be equally effective, and one
is not better than the other. They are
simply different tools.

Affirmations are not associated with
any religion; therefore, anyone can use
them, regardless of their beliefs.

Let's explore what mantras can do
for you!

CHAPTER

1

HOW to START?

There is no hard-and-fast rule as to when to chant mantras, but the best time is early in the morning, or just before going to sleep.

In the morning

Our minds are fresh and receptive; chanting mantras helps us prepare for the day ahead in a more conscious, mindful way.

In the evening

Chanting helps us come to terms with what happened during the day, let go of any negative emotions and thoughts, and have a good night's sleep.

Whenever you decide to chant, make sure you have a few peaceful minutes. Allow no distractions. It should be a dedicated time for chanting and meditation.

You don't have to chant for hours –
certainly not in the beginning. Start
with just a couple of minutes each day,
and gradually increase the amount of
time you spend with your mantras.

The ideal length of time to chant each
day is as long as you can hold your
attention from wandering off, whether
it is two minutes, or two hours.

If you are able to, create a special space for chanting. It could be a corner of a room, or the space in front of your altar, if you have one.

Having a designated space reinforces the idea that chanting is a meaningful, spiritual activity that is different from mundane, everyday life.

Decorate your sacred space with things that make you happy and remind you of your goal. Religious items, candles, and motivational quotes are all great things to have.

You could use white noise or soothing music in the background to help you focus and filter out noise from outside. Make sure it doesn't take your focus away from chanting.

Before chanting, light a candle and some incense sticks to signal that what is going to happen has spiritual significance.

This creates a solemn atmosphere, and helps you settle into a slower, meditative mindset required for chanting.

Hindus offer the candle and the incense, along with fresh fruit, water, and flowers, to gods. They place these items on the altar while chanting mantras and singing devotional songs.

If you would like to do this, make sure you are wearing clean clothes and wash your hands before starting.

The ideal time to do devotional chanting is just after you take a shower in the morning.

Settle down in a comfortable position. The best one is the lotus position, known as Padmasana, but any position is good as long as your back is straight.

This is important for the energy you create to be able to travel along your spine and your chakras.

Take a few deep breaths, and exhale slowly. Focus on your mantra, and your intention when chanting it.

If you are using a religious mantra, think of your god or goddess, and how grateful you are for him or her.

If you are not religious, think of all the things you are grateful for in your life.

Chant your mantras out loud

Advanced practitioners may chant silently in their minds, but saying the mantras out loud helps to maintain focus. It is also beneficial for your surroundings to share the vibrations you create.

Mantras have the power to clear negative energy from spaces, too.

Find a rhythm that feels right to you. Remember to focus on the mantra's meaning or intention while chanting.

You might want to use a mala or a rosary to keep track of how many mantras you have chanted, or to give you a target.

The ideal number of times for traditional mantras is 108, the sacred number of Hinduism. You can find shorter malas, or malas that mark every 27th bead with a different textured one. You can start with fewer, or do more, as you feel able to.

Remember – rushing through a rosary just for the sake of it doesn't have as many benefits as slowly, deliberately chanting.

The best material for a mala is wood, or rudraksh seeds, but the most important thing to consider is whether it feels good to hold it.

If you can't find a mala you like, you can make your own at home. String 108 beads of your choice on a thread, and add a bigger bead at the end to mark where you need to start over.

Using a mala is not only practical for keeping count and focus through the hand's motion, but it is also beneficial from an acupressure point of view.

There is a specific way you have to count your beads, which stimulates the pressure points associated with stabilizing blood pressure, as well as the pineal gland, which is associated with the third eye chakra.

Hold your mala in your right hand.

Start counting from the first small bead next to the big, head bead in the middle.

Hold the first bead between your thumb and your middle finger.

Your index finger should be held on the side to avoid touching the mala.

The index finger is considered unclean, and you want to keep your energy as pure as possible while chanting.

The index finger is associated with the pressure points of relieving constipation and diarrhoea, which is not useful when trying to meditate.

Holding the first bead this way, chant your mantra.

When you are done, move to the next bead on the mala, and chant again.

When you reach the end of the mala, you can simply start over, going in the opposite direction.

If you don't like the idea of using a mala or a rosary, you could set an alarm to let you know when it is time to stop chanting.

Choose a soothing tone for the alarm and keep the volume low to avoid shaking yourself out of meditation at the end of your session.

Never rush chanting

There is no point saying 108 mantras if you mindlessly rush through them and have another dozen things on your mind you need to get done afterwards.

Find the time every day, even if it is only five minutes, to chant in peace.

To choose a mantra, you need to decide what you want to achieve by chanting.

In this book, you will find mantras for the most common human desires: peace, love, health, spiritual growth, self-esteem, financial stability, and knowledge.

When you choose a mantra, try to find a recording of it online. Learn how to pronounce each sound. This is especially important with Sanskrit mantras.

Make sure you listen to native speakers when you choose a mantra that is not in your own language.

did you

KNOW?

The number

108

is sacred in many
Eastern religions,
and it is not
a coincidence.

The diameter of the Sun
is **108** times that of the Earth.

The average distance between
the Earth and the Sun is **108** times
the Sun's diameter.

The average distance between
the Earth and the Moon is **108** times
the Moon's diameter.

108 might be the key ratio
to habitable planets, and sages in
ancient times realized the
number's significance.

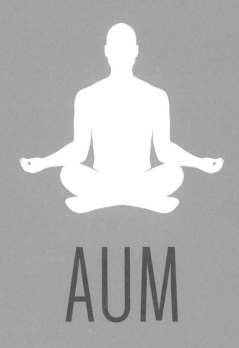

AUM

Aum is the very first
mantra.

In fact, it is the
very first sound
that came to be,
and the source of all
other sounds that
came after.

Abrahamic religions say that "In the beginning was the Word, and the Word was with God, and the Word was God".

Similarly, Hindus believe that in the beginning there was nothing created, only Lord Vishnu existed, sleeping in the cosmic ocean.

When Vishnu came to consciousness, the first sound that rippled through the Universe and created the intricate patterns that gave birth to everything else was Aum.

Chanting Aum calms your mind, relaxes your body, and uplifts your spirit.

Its vibrations travel through your chakra system. It gives your body a gentle massage, while realigning your energy centres.

It is a healing and cleansing mantra that anyone can use, regardless of religion.

While chanting Aum, focus on your own voice.

Note how its vibration starts from your abdomen, travels up your chest, and reverberates in your oral and nasal cavity.

Aum is the easiest mantra to learn

Take a deep breath and, breathing out of your stomach, say "Aaaah".

Still using the same breath, gradually close your mouth; that is where the U sound comes from.

Finally, close your lips and let the
M vibrate in your mouth.

Chant this mantra before prayer,
studies, sleeping, or whenever you
need to calm down and focus.

did you

KNOW?

Aum is the symbol of Hinduism.

The three sounds making it up
are associated with the three main
gods of Hinduism.

A for Brahma, the Creator.

U for Vishnu, the Preserver.

M for Shiva, the Destroyer.

Hindus say Aum before every prayer and recitation, and when children learn to write, the Aum symbol is the first thing they draw to make their studies auspicious.

CHAPTER

2

MUDRAS
and ASANAS

Along with your voice, it can be really beneficial to utilize your whole body when chanting.

ASANAS

There are a number of positions, or asanas, that are traditionally used for chanting, and that can aid with relaxation and focus.

These vary by difficulty, but don't worry if you don't feel comfortable with any of them. You will feel the benefits of chanting, even if you are simply sitting on a chair, or lying in bed while doing it.

Listen to what your body tells you, and never force any of these positions. If you have health problems, please consult your doctor before attempting these asanas.

SUKHASANA

This sitting position's name literally means "the easy pose". Sit cross-legged on the floor. Make sure your back is straight, and turn your face straight forward, or slightly upwards. Place your hands on your knees in your preferred mudra (see page 66), or just rest your hands on your knees while you chant.

This position is not recommended if you have arthritis or joint pains, especially in your leg.

PADMASANA

This sitting position's name means "lotus pose". Start by sitting cross-legged, then place each foot on the thigh of the other leg. Make sure your back is straight and you face straight forward, or slightly upwards.

This might be the standard position we associate with meditation, but it is not the easiest one, and requires some practice before it becomes comfortable.

You could consider starting with a half lotus position, where you only place one foot on the opposite thigh, and let the other stay in a basic cross-legged position.

Do not force it, or you could risk serious injury to your knees.

This position is not recommended if you have hip, knee, or ankle problems, or pain in your lower back.

VAJRASANA

This sitting position's name means "diamond", or "thunderbolt pose". It is a kneeling position with both legs folded under yourself.

Make sure to keep your back straight and face forward. Rest your hands on your knees, or keep them on your thighs in your preferred mudra.

This position is not recommended if you have poor circulation in your legs, joint problems, suffer from digestive issues such as a hernia or ulcers, or if you have pain in your lower back.

SAVASANA

This lying position's name means "corpse pose". Lie down on your back on a firm, but not uncomfortably hard surface – a carpeted floor, or a yoga mat on the ground should be fine. Keep your back straight but relaxed. Let your legs and hands extend away from your body, and turn your palms upwards.

There are no counterindications for this pose, but be careful not to fall asleep while chanting.

VRIKSHASANA

This standing position's name means "tree pose". While standing up, keep your left leg straight and bend your right leg. Place your right sole on the inner thigh of your left leg. Find your balance and keep your back straight.

Now, lift your hands and, keeping your elbows straight, join your palms above your head. Keep your face looking straight.

Alternatively, join your hands in front of your chest in a prayer, or namaste position.

If you need help with your balance, you could start by holding on to the back of a chair until you are confident.

This position is not recommended if you have blood pressure problems, migraines, or insomnia, or if you suffer from vertigo.

MUDRAS

Mudras are hand gestures and positions that help energy flow through specific parts of the body.

Each mudra has a specific meaning, and has different effects on the body and mind.

When practicing with mudras, press the fingers lightly together. There shouldn't be high pressure in your hands, but the shape of the mudra should be maintained during the whole duration of your chanting.

Do your chosen mudra as well as you can, depending on your ability. Never force any of them, or you could injure the joints in your hands.

Take short breaks if you need to, and return to the mudra when you are ready.

the NAMASTE, or ATMANJALI mudra

Join your palms in a prayer position. Lightly press your palms together, but don't use force. Keeping your fingers joined, create a slight distance between your palms, as if you are holding something between them. Hold this mudra in front of your chest, or above your head. The Atmanjali mudra helps to regulate emotions, and brings gratitude and mindfulness to your life.

the DHYAN mudra

With your palms facing upwards, place your right hand on your left palm. Join the tips of your thumbs creating a triangle-shaped space between your palms and thumbs.

The Dhyan mudra can help in any healing process, and brings inner peace and deep concentration.

the USHAS mudra

This mudra has a slight variation depending on whether the practitioner is male or female.

Start with your palms facing you, and intertwine your fingers. Male practitioners place their right thumb on top of the left, gently pressing it.

Female practitioners place their left thumb on top, pressing gently on the right.

The Ushas mudra can help to improve hormonal problems, and ushers in creativity and new ideas, as well as the motivation to bring those ideas to fruition.

the GANESH mudra

Clasp your hands in front of your chest, gently letting them pull against each other, but not releasing the mudra.

The Ganesh mudra strengthens the heart and the upper body, and gives courage and compassion.

the GYAN mudra

Join the tips of your thumb and your index finger, and keep the other three fingers straight. Do this with both hands.

The Gyan mudra helps to improve focus and memory, and increases clarity.

the PRAN mudra

Join the tip of your thumb, your ring finger and your pinkie finger. The other two fingers should be held straight. Do this with both hands.

The Pran mudra helps to boost immunity and health, and awakens strength.

the APAN mudra

Join the tip of your thumb, your middle finger and your ring finger. Your index and pinkie fingers should be held straight. Do this with both hands.

The Apan mudra helps with digestive and metabolism issues, and allows you to let go of what doesn't serve you anymore.

the RUDRA mudra

Join the tips of the thumb, the ring finger and the index finger. The middle and pinkie fingers should be held straight. Do this with both hands.

The Rudra mudra improves circulation, brings clarity, and aids with decision-making and taking control of your life.

the SHUNYA mudra

Bend your middle finger, and touch
the base of your thumb, just where
it meets the fleshy part of your palm.
Place your thumb above it to hold it
in place. The other fingers should be
held straight.

The Shunya mudra can alleviate
hearing- and balance-related
problems, and improves intuition and
introspection.

CHAPTER
3

HINDU
MANTRAS

In this chapter you will find Hindu mantras that people use in daily puja (worship), and ones that are used for special occasions and for specific reasons.

Mantras have been a powerful tool in Hinduism for thousands of years.

In Hindu rituals and ceremonies, the chanting of mantras is a means of attracting positive energy and blessings.

In meditation and yoga practices, chanting is often used as a method for focusing the mind and accessing deeper levels of consciousness.

the GAYATRI mantra

"Aum Bhur Bhuva Svaha
(Aumm Bhoor Bhoo-va Su-va-ha)

Tat Savitur Varenyam
(Tat Sa-vee-toor Var-ayn-yam)

Bhargo Devasya Dhimahi
(Bar-go Day-vas-ya Dhee-ma-hee)

Dhiyo Yo Nah Prachodayat"
(Dhee-yo Yo Nah Pra-cho-da-yaat)

The Gayatri Mantra is one of the most widely used mantras in the world.

Originating from the Rigveda, one of the oldest Hindu scriptures written around 1500 BCE, it is one of the most sacred and powerful of all Hindu mantras.

It means:

"Aum, salutations to the three dimensions, the Underworld, Earth, and the Heavens.

May the divine light of the rising sun illuminate our minds and give us true knowledge."

Chant this mantra to help you with studies, clear thinking, or before work to aid you in concentration.

It clears negative thoughts, and helps you maintain a healthy relationship with others.

The mantra's vibrations aid the functions of the lungs and the heart.

The best time to chant this mantra is early in the morning when the night darkness has passed but the sun has still not risen, or late evening after the sun has set and the night darkness has not yet arrived.

did you

KNOW?

The Gayatri mantra is also called the **Savitr mantra,** after the god of the rising sun, Savitr.

Gayatri is the verse form this mantra is written in.

It has such great importance that the mantra is personified as Goddess Gayatri.

You can find this mantra written on the belt of George Harrison's statue in Liverpool, UK.

the MAHA MRITYUNJAYA mantra

"Aum trayambakam yajaamahe
sugandhim pushtivardhanam

Urvaarukamiva bandhanaan mrityor
muksheeya maamritaat Aum"

It means:

"Aum. We worship the three-eyed lord (Lord Shiva), who is fragrant and who nurtures all beings.

As the ripened cucumber is freed from the vine, may he liberate us from death and rebirth. Aum."

This mantra is dedicated to Lord Shiva, the Destroyer god from the Hindu Trinity. Lord Shiva eliminates ignorance, and brings transformation to the world.

The mantra originates in the Rigveda and, just like the Gayatri mantra, forms part of many Hindus' daily rituals.

Maha Mrityunjaya mantra means
'the Great Death-Defeating mantra'.

It is chanted for good health,
protection, enlightenment, and for us
to be freed from the cycle of death
and rebirth. It removes fear from
those who chant it. It eases
the passage of the dying, and gives
solace to those who are left behind.

Its vibrations support the heart, and
propagate mental wellbeing.

the MAHAMANTRA

"Hare Rama Hare Rama
Rama Rama Hare Hare
Hare Krishna Hare Krishna
Krishna Krishna Hare Hare"

It is the repetition of three names of the same deity, Lord Krishna.

Hare means Lord Vishnu, the Preserver god of the Hindu Trinity.

Krishna and Rama are the avatars of Lord Vishnu, who is, in the Hare Krishna movement, the avatar of the supreme god, Krishna.

This is the mantra you may have heard ISCKON devotees chant on the street.

It first appears in the Kali Santarana Upanishad, and is said to remove all negative effects of the Kali Yuga. It brings inner peace, joy, and connection to the higher self and God.

It helps us to see beyond the material vices of current society, and gives those who chant it a deeper, truer satisfaction.

did you
KNOW?

This mantra can be heard in the movie *Hair*.

The Mahamantra is part of George Harrison's song "My Sweet Lord".

the GANESHA mantra

"Aum Shri Ganeshaya Namah"

This mantra is dedicated to Lord Ganesha, the elephant-headed remover of obstacles, god of knowledge, the son of Lord Shiva and Goddess Parvati.

It means:

"I bow to Lord Ganesha."

It draws on Lord Ganesha's vibrations, which are curiosity, determination, and success.

This mantra brings determination. It makes the mind more receptive to knowledge. It helps to focus on studies and the use of knowledge to solve difficult situations in any area of life.

It improves memory and focus, and, along with medication, can help relieve the symptoms of executive dysfunction and ADHD.

the SHIVA mantra

"Aum Namah Shivaya"

This mantra is dedicated to Lord Shiva.
It is easy to learn and pronounce,
therefore it may be more suitable for
beginners.

It simply means:

"I bow to Lord Shiva."

It draws on Lord Shiva's vibration,
which is unlimited strength and
belief in yourself.

The Shiva mantra relieves stress, fear, and anxiety. It helps mental health, and gives positive emotions and thoughts to those who chant it.

It has a positive effect on blood circulation, and it can aid medication to prevent stroke and other circulatory diseases.

It does not substitute medication; rather, it works hand in hand with it.

the DURGA mantra

"Aum Dum Durgaye Namaha"

This mantra is dedicated to Goddess Durga, the goddess of strength, protection, motherhood, war, and destruction.

She is the wife of Lord Shiva, and the mother of Ganesha, the god of knowledge, and Kartikey, the god of war.

It means:

"I bow to Goddess Durga."

The seed mantra Dum stands for the essence of Goddess Durga, and adds extra power to the mantra.

It draws on Goddess Durga's vibrations, which are motherly nurturing and protection, and righteous rage and the destruction of evil.

This mantra eliminates all evil from the chanter's life, whatever form it may take. It brings health, financial success, and removes or mitigates the effect of negative people and energy from one's life.

It has a positive effect on the metabolism, and increases overall bodily strength.

the VISHNU mantra

"Aum Namo Narayanaya"

This mantra is dedicated to
Lord Vishnu, the Preserver god of the
Hindu Trinity.

It means:

"I bow to Lord Vishnu."

Lord Vishnu is called Narayana when he is in his yogic slumber on the cosmic ocean.

It draws on Lord Vishnu's vibration, which is a strong sense of duty, protection, and vitality.

This mantra brings peace and protection to those who chant it.

It helps the seeker on their journey to enlightenment, and quietens the ego and material attachments.

It helps to relax the mind and the body, brings a sense of security, and can relieve insomnia and depression.

the LAKSHMI mantra

*"Om Hring Kling
MahaLakshmyai Namah"*

This mantra is dedicated to Goddess Lakshmi, the goddess of wealth and abundance, both in the spiritual and material meaning of the words.

It means:

"I bow to Goddess Lakshmi."

The two seed mantras, Hring and Kling, strengthen the effect of this mantra. Hring is for attaining higher knowledge and wisdom, and Kling is for helping you attract what you desire.

It draws on Goddess Lakshmi's vibrations, which is abundance in every sense of the word.

This mantra brings success, abundance, and wealth, and an overall feeling of good health.

the SARASWATI
mantra

*"Aum Shreem Bhreem
Saraswathaye Namaha"*

This mantra is dedicated to Saraswati,
the goddess of arts, speech, and
wisdom.

Saraswati is the wife of Brahma, the creator god of the Hindu Trinity, and the mother of the Vedas and the divine sage Narad.

It means:

"I bow to Goddess Saraswati."

The seed mantras Shreem and Bhreem request an abundance of Saraswati's blessings.

It draws on Goddess Saraswati's vibrations, which are creativity, beauty, and knowledge.

This mantra brings creative ideas, inspiration, guidance, and humbleness to learn.

FOOD BLESSING PRAYER

*"Brahmarpaṇaṃ brahma haviḥ
brahmagnau brahmaṇa hutam*

*brahmaiva tena gaṃtavyam
brahmakarma samaādhina"*

This is not a mantra, but a prayer, a
verse from the Bhagavad Gita.

It is to be chanted before eating, to bless the food.

It means:

"Any means of offering is Brahman, the oblation is Brahman, the fire in which the offering is made is Brahman, and the one who offers is Brahman.

Such a person who abides in Brahman indeed gains Brahman."

This prayer is dedicated to Goddess Annapurna, a form of Goddess Durga, who is the goddess of food and nourishment.

It purifies the food, so that it nourishes not only the body, but also the soul.

It also clears our minds to be able to accept and take the purified nourishment in its full potency.

These are the most important and most popular mantras dedicated to gods in the Hindu religion.

Other popular gods include Hanuman, Kuber, Surya, Agni, Shani, and Vishvakarma.

If you have a goal you'd like to achieve that is not listed in this book, you could try to look for the god of that thing, and search for their mantra.

did you
KNOW?

In this chapter, we have covered the mantras for two of the Hindu Trinity, and all three of the trinity's female counterparts.

But the third god, **Lord Brahma, the Creator,** is forbidden to be worshipped.

Four different stories why this is, all of them citing the god's immoral behaviour as the reason for the ban.

Brahma does have a mantra, and has been known to bestow great boons on his worshippers, who were – more often than not – demons who wanted to take over the world.

CHAPTER

4

non-religious

SANSKRIT MANTRAS

Sanskrit is one of the oldest classical languages in the world and is widely used as a ceremonial and ritual language in Hindu and Buddhist mantras.

the PAVAMANA

mantra

"Asato Ma Sadgamaya

Tamaso Ma Jyotirgamaya

Mrtyormamrtam Gamaya"

It means:

*"From the unreal, lead me
to the real!*

*From the darkness, lead me
to the light!*

*From death, lead me
to immortality!"*

This mantra traditionally has been used at the beginning of the Soma Sacrifice. Soma is the god of the Moon, and self-realized immortality.

Today it is chanted as a cleansing mantra, one to lead people to peace and moksha. It can be chanted on your own for finding inner peace, or before any event for its success.

did you

KNOW?

This mantra has been
worked into the
Matrix: Revolutions
and
Battlestar Galactica
soundtracks.

MANTRA for
HAPPINESS

"Lokah samastah sukhino bhavantu"

It means:

"May everyone in the whole world be happy."

This mantra is often chanted at the end of religious ceremonies and yoga classes. It brings contentment and joy.

"Prana mantraso ham"

It means:

"I am he/she/that."

This mantra helps the practitioner to realize their true nature: that we are all souls, all part of the same cosmic energy.

It is also used to regulate the breath in yoga practice. Inhaling, we say "Sooooo", and when exhaling, we say "Hummmmm", focusing on the meaning of the mantra, as well as on our breathing.

This mantra can also help with visualization. Concentrate on the mindset you would like to achieve: confidence, health, joy, success. Then chant this mantra while visualizing yourself being what you want to be.

PEACE MANTRA

"Aum dyauh shantir antariksham

Shanti prithvi shantir apah

Shantir osadhayah shantih vanaspatayah

Shantir vishvedevah shantir brahma

Shantih sarvam shantih shantir eva

Shantih sa ma shantir edhi

Aum shanti shanti shanti"

It means:

"Aum. May peace radiate in the sky and in space everywhere.

May peace reign all over this Earth, in water and in all the Earth's plants.

May peace be with all souls, may peace be in the whole of creation,

May everyone and everything always exist in peace.

Let there be peace, peace and peace alone, Aum."

This mantra is usually recited at the end of a function or ritual, to send everyone on their way in peace.

It is found in the Yajurveda, and is around 3,000 years old.

SHORT PEACE MANTRA

"Aum Shanti Shanti Shanti"

It means:

"Let there be peace, peace, peace."

This mantra brings peace, too, but instead of dividing your focus between the external and the internal world, it concentrates solely on inner peace.

It releases the mind from reactions to external stimuli, material desires, and aversions.

When chanting from the heart,
it creates a stable, level mind,
and helps the chanter to realize
we are all manifestations of the
same cosmic energy.

CHAPTER

5

BUDDHIST MANTRAS

"Aum mani padme hum"

This is one of the most popular and well-known Buddhist mantras.

Its meaning is debated by scholars, but the most probable literal translation is:

"Praise to the jewel in the lotus."

Lotus flowers are sacred symbols of enlightenment and purity in Indian religions, because lotuses are usually found in swamps, but the flower is not tarnished by the dirt it grows from.

This mantra brings enlightenment. It purifies the mind, body, and soul of those who chant it, and brings inner peace and contentment.

*"Gate gate paragate
parasamgate bodhi svaha"*

It means:

*"Gone, gone, absolutely gone
beyond enlightenment,
so be it!"*

This mantra concludes the Heart Stotra, Prajnaparamita Hridaya.

The poem talks about how everything we can see is an illusion, and says that by chanting this mantra, we will be able to cut through this illusion, and reach enlightenment.

"Aum Vasudhare Swaha"

It means:

"Salutations to Lord Vasudhara"

This is a mantra that brings wealth – spiritual or material. Although Buddhism teaches detachment from material vices, it also recognizes that without money, nothing can happen in this plane of existence.

To help devotees achieve a more secure financial status so they are able to focus on spirituality, the Buddha shared this mantra, dedicated to the deity of wealth, Vasudhara, or, as she is called in Tibet, Norgyun.

She is often compared to the Hindu Goddess Lakshmi.

"Aum muni muni mahamuni shakyamuniye svaha"

It means:

"Salutations to the sage, the great wise Shakyamuni sage."

This is the first mantra of the Buddha, Prince Siddharta Gautama.

He was born a prince into the Shakyamuni clan, hence the name in the mantra. His father tried to shelter him from all suffering in life, but the inevitable happened when Siddharta went on a chariot ride around his city.

He saw hunger, illness, and death,
and it influenced him so deeply,
that he embarked on a journey to
enlightenment.

The word Buddha
is a denominative;
it means
"the enlightened *one*".

CHAPTER

6

MONO-
THEISTIC
RELIGIONS

While Hinduism and Buddhism are very open religions with an extremely broad spectrum of followers, monotheistic religions are more exclusive to their practitioners.

If you are not a follower of one of the following religions, you might want to check with a rabbi, priest or imam first, whether it is okay for you to use these religious chants. It may be perceived as cultural appropriation, or as being disrespectful.

Being mindful of peoples' religious sentiments is the decent thing to do before adopting any of these chants.

The following chants have been added with this in mind, and assume that the chanter is a practitioner of the given religion.

HEBREW
CHANTS

the NAME of GOD

"Yod-Heh, Vav-Heh"

Just like So Hum, this mantra is used along with the rhythm of your breathing: the first two letters while breathing in, the last two while breathing out.

It represents the Tetragrammaton, the name of God.

If you are not comfortable with uttering this name, you could chant other names the Torah uses for God.

These include El Shaddai, which means "The Nurturer", or Shechinah, which is God's presence in the world.

Arguably, this isn't pronouncing God's name in vain, because you are meditating on Him, calling Him to see and bless you with His presence; you are working on getting even closer to Him in soul.

Modern branches of Judaism permit taking God's name in this way, but if you are unsure, it is always best to check with your Rabbi.

OH LORD, HERE I AM!

"Adonai Hinani"

When God called Moses from the burning bush on Mount Sinai, this is what Moses replied.

It doesn't only mean "Here I am" in the physical sense. It is also a submission to God in body and soul.

You open yourself up to Him, and let His love and protection fill you with its warmth.

Chant this in the morning and before sleep, and whenever you need strength and reassurance.

FOOD
BLESSING
prayers

Jewish people say prayers every time they eat, even if it is only a snack. The following are different types of blessings, for different types of food.

For food that does not grow from the ground, such as meat, eggs, or dairy

"Barukh ata Adonai Eloheinu melekh ha'olam shehakol niyah bidvaro"

It means:

"Blessed are You, Lord our God, Ruler of the universe, at whose word all came to be."

For bread

"Barukh ata Adonai Eloheinu melekh ha'olam hamotzi lehem min ha'aretz"

It means:

"Blessed are You, Lord our God, Ruler of the universe, who brings forth bread from the Earth."

For wine
(also applies for grape juice)

*"Barukh ata Adonai Eloheinu
melekh ha'olam borei
p'ri hagafen"*

It means:

*"Blessed are You,
Lord our God, Ruler of the
universe, who creates the fruit
of the vine."*

For fruit

*"Barukh ata Adonai Eloheinu
melekh ha'olam borei
p'ri ha'eitz"*

It means:

*"Blessed are You,
Lord our God, Ruler of the
universe, who creates the fruit
of the tree."*

For Vegetables

"Barukh ata Adonai Eloheinu melekh ha'olam borei p'ri ha'adamah"

It means:

"Blessed are You, Lord our God, Ruler of the universe, who creates the fruit of the ground."

For grains

"Barukh ata Adonai Eloheinu melekh ha'olam borei minei mezonot"

It means:

"Blessed are You, Lord our God, Ruler of the universe, who creates varieties of nourishment."

If you are eating a main course with meat, you should use the first prayer; if your meal contains bread, then the second one can be used to cover everything.

Wine always receives its own prayer, no matter what else is on the table.

CHRISTIAN CHANTS

MARANATHA

This is an early Christian mantra, found in the New Testament.

The word is in Aramaic, the language Jesus would have spoken.

The catechism of the Catholic Church translates it to:

"Come, oh Lord."

Use this mantra like So Hum. Divide its syllables and say them while breathing in and out.

ma – breath in; **ra** – breath out; **na** – breath in; **tha** – breath out.

Chant this in the morning and before sleep, and whenever you need strength and reassurance.

ROSARY prayers

Many Christians use rosaries and repeat prayers to God, Jesus, the Virgin Mary or one of the many saints and angels.

While these are not exactly mantras, they can have the same psychological effect – i.e. bringing you closer to God, or helping you reach a certain mindset.

Compassion, forgiveness, courage;
even lost items have a patron saint
– St Anthony of Padua can help in
recovering lost items.

Choose a prayer that fits your goal,
and repeat it from your heart, paying
attention to the meaning of the words
you say.

OUR FATHER

Our Father, who art in heaven,
hallowed be Thy name:
Thy kingdom come:
Thy will be done on Earth as
it is in heaven.
Give us this day our daily bread:
and forgive us our trespasses
as we forgive those who
trespass against us.
Do not let us fall into temptation,
but deliver us from evil. Amen.

HAIL MARY

*Hail Mary, full of grace,
the Lord is with thee:
blessed art thou among
women, and blessed is the
fruit of thy womb, Jesus.
Holy Mary, Mother of God,
pray for us sinners,
now and at the hour of our
death. Amen.*

GLORY BE

*Glory be to the Father,
and to the Son and to the
Holy Spirit.*

*As it was in the beginning,
is now and ever shall
be, world without end.
Amen.*

FOOD BLESSING

prayer

*Bless us, O Lord, and these
Thy gifts which we are
about to receive through
Thy bounty.
Through Christ our Lord
we pray.
Amen.*

MUSLIM
CHANTS

In Islam, Muslims chant the Asma-ul-Husna, the 99 names of God, while contemplating His attributes.

All names have a meaning, and different names have different benefits when chanting.

the TAKBIR

"Allahu Akbar"

It means:

"Allah is the Greatest."

Muslims use it before and after prayer, and any time of the day to remember Allah and His merciful nature.

It is not a battle cry, as it is often portrayed in the media, but a praise to Allah.

the PRAYER of BEGINNINGS

"Bismillah Hir Rahman Nir Rahim"

It means:

"In the name of Allah, the most gracious and merciful."

This prayer is recited before starting anything, be it work, prayer, or a meal. This prayer ensures that whatever you do, you do it with clear intentions, in the name of God.

CHAPTER

7

AFFIRMATIONS

Affirmations can be used regardless of your cultural or religious heritage. They are simple yet effective statements that aim to put you in the right mindset for the day ahead.

On the following pages, you will find affirmations for any occasion, including ones used by celebrities, but feel free to make up your own!

How to write your own affirmation

Affirmations tailored to your personal circumstances are the most effective.

Be as specific as you need to be:

"I will accept the red light at the big junction I always get caught in with grace and good humour"

is even more effective than

"I will stay calm all morning".

Use positive statements and avoid using negation in your affirmation.

For example:

"I will not get angry today"

is less effective than

"I will remain calm and understanding all day".

Jordan Peterson has a great way to explain why. He says, tell someone NOT to imagine an elephant. Now all they can think about is the elephant. But if you tell people to think of a tiger, and you don't even mention the elephant, it will not come to their mind that easily.

You can absolutely use verses from scriptures as affirmations, or make up your own. "God loves me", "Goddess Lakshmi protects my business", or "The muses guide my pen as I write my poetry" are all beautiful ways to reassure yourself.

AFFIRMATIONS
for LOVE

I am loving.

I am loved.

I am worthy of love.

I am open to new love.

I accept it with a clear heart and mind.

I attract new, honest love.

I show my love to those dear to me.

I express my love and appreciation
every day.

AFFIRMATIONS for SELF-WORTH

I am worthy.

I am capable.

I am strong and determined.

I am smart.

I am beautiful as I am.

I love my body.

I matter, I have the right to shine.

I walk and talk my truth.

I surround myself with people who love and support me.

I love and support people.

AFFIRMATIONS
for SUCCESS

I attract success.

I attract wealth.

I attract people who support me and whom I can support.

I attract great opportunities and connections.

I am goal-oriented and determined.

I create the life I want to live.

I work for my success, and I enjoy every second of it.

I am steadfast in the face of hardships.

I am stubborn and strong.

This is my calling, and I follow it to the end.

"*Nothing can dim the light that shines from within.*"

MAYA ANGELOU